LINCOLN

on Law,
Leadership,
and Life

Jonathan W. White

Published by Cumberland House, an imprint of Sourcebooks, Inc.
P.O. Box 4410, Naperville, Illinois 60567-4410
(630) 961-3900
Fax: (630) 961-2168
www.sourcebooks.com

Library of Congress Cataloging-in-Publication data is on file with the publisher.

Printed and bound in the China.
NRD 10 9 8 7 6 5 4 3 2

For my prelaw students at
Christopher Newport University

When Abraham Lincoln left Springfield, Illinois, for the White House in February 1861, he turned to his law partner, William H. Herndon, and said, "Billy, over sixteen years together, and we have not had a cross word during all that time, have we?"

"Not one," replied Herndon.

"Don't take the sign down, Billy; let it swing, that our clients may understand that the election of a President makes no change in the firm of Lincoln and Herndon. If I live, I'm coming back, and we will go right on practicing law as if nothing had ever happened."

TABLE OF CONTENTS

INTRODUCTION

IN OCTOBER 1857, Abraham Lincoln defended a seventy-year-old woman named Melissa Goings, who was on trial for the murder of her husband. Melissa and her seventy-seven-year-old husband, Roswell, had apparently been living "rather disagreeably" for some time. On April 14, 1857, the two got into a fight over whether or not to open a window. Roswell allegedly tried to choke Melissa; she therefore claimed to be acting in self-defense when she whacked him over the head with a stick of firewood. "I expect she has killed me," Roswell told a neighbor after the scuffle, adding, "If I get over it I will have revenge." He died four days later.

As the trial got under way on October 10 at a small county courthouse near Peoria, Illinois, Mrs. Goings was nowhere to be found. A court officer accused Lincoln of encouraging his client to escape, but Lincoln denied the charge. "I didn't run her off," he told the court. "She wanted to know where she could get a drink of water, and I told her there was mighty good water in Tennessee."

ABRAHAM LINCOLN WAS a talented, practical lawyer. In fact, Lincoln's success as a politician and statesman was rooted in his experience as an attorney. His presidency was plagued by constitutional problems and legal crises. Yet he deftly led the nation through a great civil war—our nation's most divisive constitutional conflict—in large measure as a sensible prairie lawyer in the White House.

As a young man, Lincoln taught himself the law. He quickly became one of the most prominent attorneys in Illinois, handling every type of case imaginable—murder trials and other criminal proceedings, bankruptcy filings, divorces, larceny, trespasses, ejectments, railroads and big business, libel and slander, civil disputes, and debt collection. Lots of debt collection. But Lincoln did not deal only with trials in the lower courts. He also argued nearly 350 cases before the Illinois Supreme Court and one case before the U.S. Supreme Court in Washington, DC.

Young men in Illinois often looked to Lincoln for insight into how to become an attorney (only men could practice law in those days). Through letters, speeches, and informal conversations, Lincoln gave them advice based on his experiences. Lincoln's wit and wisdom are still relevant today for both aspiring lawyers and practicing attorneys. Indeed, while the legal profession in the United States has changed in many ways over the past century and a half, many of Lincoln's principles are timeless.

In a larger sense, Lincoln's advice for lawyers is also relevant for people who work outside the legal profession. As we will see, Lincoln believed the highest duty of a lawyer was to be a peacemaker in his community. Therefore, any reader who deals with interpersonal conflict can learn from Lincoln's insights. Indeed, Lincoln's lessons for attorneys can apply to almost any walk of life.

The words in the chapters that follow come directly from Lincoln and his friends. Many come from Lincoln's own correspondence. Others are recollections of those who knew him. Some of his friends' stories may be exaggerated or embellished—some may even have been fabricated or misremembered when they were recalled so many years after

Lincoln's death. But perhaps we can learn as much about what it means to be a good lawyer from the myths and legends about Lincoln as we can from the reality.

THIS DAGUERREOTYPE, TAKEN IN ABOUT 1846 WHEN LINCOLN WAS ELECTED TO CONGRESS, DEPICTS THE YOUNG LAWYER IN SPRINGFIELD, ILLINOIS. IT IS THE EARLIEST KNOWN PHOTOGRAPH OF THE FUTURE PRESIDENT. COURTESY OF THE LIBRARY OF CONGRESS.

CHAPTER 1

"IF YOU WISH TO BE A LAWYER"

Lincoln's Advice to Aspiring Lawyers

IN THE NINETEENTH century, it was much more common for an aspiring lawyer to "read law" in the office of a practicing attorney than to attend law school. Law schools were few and far between, especially on the frontier. In Chicago, for example, only five of the forty-four attorneys who practiced between 1830 and 1850 had attended law school.

In the mid-1830s, Whig attorney and state legislator John Todd Stuart encouraged young Abraham Lincoln to become a lawyer. Lincoln started his study of the law in New Salem,

Illinois, by borrowing law books and reading them. "He borrowed books of Stuart, took them home with him, and went at it in good earnest," stated an 1860 campaign biography. Another campaign document described Lincoln's intense study of the great eighteenth-century English jurist William Blackstone:

He bought an old copy of Blackstone, one day, at auction, in Springfield, and on his return to New Salem, attacked the work with characteristic energy. His favorite place of study was a wooded knoll near New Salem, where he threw himself under a wide-spreading oak, and expansively made a reading desk of the hillside. Here he would pore over Blackstone day after day, shifting his position as the sun rose and sank, so as to keep in the shade, and utterly unconscious of everything but the principles of common law. People went by, and he took no account of them; the salutations of acquaintances were returned with silence, or a vacant stare; and altogether the manner of the absorbed student was not unlike that of one distraught.

This story was corroborated years later by a New Salem man who recalled seeing Lincoln study Blackstone:

When he began to study law he would go day after day for weeks and sit under an oak tree on [a] hill near [New] Salem, and read—[he] moved round [the] tree to keep in [the] shade—was so absorbed that people said he was crazy.

Lincoln was admitted to the Illinois bar in 1836 and began practicing in 1837. Over the ensuing years, he built a reputation as a skillful attorney. Aspiring lawyers in Illinois often looked to Lincoln as a potential teacher, and he received many letters from young men who desired to read law in his office. The life of a frontier lawyer was hard, though. Lincoln spent many weeks away from home each year traveling in the Eighth Judicial Circuit, arguing cases in county courthouses throughout central Illinois. Most of the time, Lincoln declined to allow the aspirants to study under him. Instead, he sent them brief notes, recommending what they could do to become successful lawyers.

On October 23, 1855, a nineteen-year-old boy from Beardstown, Illinois, named Isham Reavis, wrote to Lincoln, asking to read law in his Springfield office. Lincoln was too busy traveling to take on a student, but he replied to Reavis's letter on November 5, 1855, with advice for how to best learn the law.

My dear Sir:

I have just reached home, and found your letter of the 23rd. ult. I am from home too much of my time, for a young man to read law with me advantageously. If you are resolutely determined to make a lawyer of yourself, the thing is more than half done already. It is but a small matter whether you read *with* any body or not. I did not read with any one. Get the books, and read and study them till, you understand them in their principal features; and that is the main thing. It is of no consequence to be in a large town while you are reading. I read at New-Salem, which never had three hundred people living in it. The *books*, and your *capacity* for understanding them, are just the same in all places. Mr. Dummer is a very clever man and an excellent lawyer (much better than I, in law-learning); and I have no doubt he will cheerfully tell you what books to read, and also loan you the books.

Always bear in mind that your own resolution to succeed, is more important than any other one thing.

Very truly Your friend

A. Lincoln

Reavis must have heeded Lincoln's advice to study with Beardstown lawyer Henry E. Dummer, a graduate of Harvard Law School. Reavis was admitted to the bar in 1857 and moved to Falls City, Nebraska, the following year, where he opened his own law office. After the Civil War, President Ulysses S. Grant appointed Reavis to serve on the supreme court of the territory of Arizona, which he did from 1869 until he resigned his seat on the bench in 1872.

On July 14, 1858, William H. Grigsby, a nineteen-year-old Missourian who had moved to Pekin, Illinois, wrote to Lincoln, requesting to study law with him. At the time, Grigsby was working for G. L. Thomas, a bookseller and stationer. Lincoln replied on August 3. His response demonstrates how many letters like these he and his law partner, William H. Herndon, were receiving.

My dear Sir:

Yours of the 14th. of July, desiring a situation in my law office, was received several days ago. My partner, Mr. Herndon, controls our office in this respect, and I have known of his declining at least a dozen applications like yours within the last three months.

If you wish to be a lawyer, attach no consequence to the *place* you are in, or the *person* you are with; but get books, sit down anywhere, and go to reading for yourself. That will make a lawyer of you quicker than any other way. Yours Respectfully,

A. Lincoln

In some instances, older men wrote letters of recommendation on behalf of young men who wished to study law. On November 29, 1858, James T. Thornton of the small village of Magnolia, Illinois, wrote to Lincoln on behalf of John H. Widmer, whom he described as "a yong man" with "rair talents" who was "desirous of pursuing the studdy of Law." At twenty-two years old, Widmer was working as a schoolteacher and county surveyor. He was good at math, had "acquired a verry perfect english education," and in his spare time read Blackstone. Thornton asked Lincoln for assistance in finding Widmer a place to study law in Springfield, concluding his letter, "I cannot speek in two flatering terms of his industry."

Lincoln replied to Thornton on December 2, 1858. He must have grown weary of responding to these letters, as is evidenced by the varying ways he spelled Widmer's name. Still, Lincoln offered encouragement and advice to the aspiring lawyer.

Dear Sir

Yours of the 29th, written in behalf of Mr. John W. Widmer, is received. I am absent altogether too much to be a suitable instructor for a law-student. When a man has reached the age that Mr. Widner has, and has already been doing for himself, my judgment is, that he reads the books for himself without an instructor. That is precisely the way I came to the law. Let Mr. Widner read Blackstone's Commentaries, Chitty's Pleading's—Greenleaf's Evidence, Story's Equity, and Story's Equity Pleading's, get a license, and go to the practice, and still keep reading. That is my judgment of the cheapest, quickest, and best way for Mr. Widner to make a lawyer of himself. Yours truly

A. Lincoln

While Lincoln usually did not have time to take students into his own law office, he would engage with those he met in other offices as he traveled the Eighth Illinois Circuit. One law student remembered that Lincoln would stop by "and take up some text-book…and give us a close and rigid examination, laughing heartily at our answers, at times; and always made the hour he spent with us interesting and instructive." Another law student had a similar recollection:

> *A student just out of college, I went into my brother's office in Bloomington, Illinois, to study law. Mr. Lincoln, as a practicing lawyer, was at that time in regular attendance at all the courts in that county. He frequently dropped into my brother's office, and there it was that I was first introduced to him, and learned to admire him for his singular but sterling traits of character and for his commanding ability. He often talked to me, and, knowing that I was fresh from college, seemed to delight in asking questions which I could not and which I am sure he never expected me to answer,*

*but which, in view of his broad knowledge
and practical experience, gave him an excellent opportunity to analyze and explain for
my benefit. It generally happened that he made
his point clear by the recital of a story which,
though sometimes a little outre, was invariably
so applicable that I never forgot it.*

Shortly before his election as president in
1860, Lincoln received a letter from a young
schoolteacher, John M. Brockman of Pleasant
Plains, Illinois, asking "the best mode of
obtaining a thorough knowledge of the law."
With just over a month until the presidential
election, Lincoln took the time to pen the following note on September 25:

J. M. Brockman, Esq.

Dear Sir: Yours of the 24th. asking "the
best mode of obtaining a thorough
knowledge of the law" is received. The

mode is very simple, though laborious, and tedious. It is only to get the books, and read, and study them carefully. Begin with Blackstone's Commentaries, and after reading it carefully through, say twice, take up Chitty's Pleading, Greenleaf's Evidence, & Story's Equity &c. in succession. Work, work, work, is the main thing. Yours very truly

A. Lincoln

The Civil War intervened, and Brockman never took Lincoln's advice. In 1861, he moved to Brownville, Nebraska, where he enlisted in the First Battalion Nebraska Cavalry (the regiment later merged with the Fifth Iowa Cavalry). After the war, Brockman took up a career as a farmer and later served two terms as a Republican in the Nebraska state legislature.

One of the most important lessons Lincoln

sought to teach young students was to never give up in the face of adversity. When George Latham, a friend of Lincoln's son Robert, was not admitted to Harvard, Lincoln wrote to him on July 22, 1860, encouraging him to press on. "I know not how to aid you, save in the assurance of one of mature age, and much severe experience, that you *can* not fail, if you resolutely determine, that you *will* not," Lincoln told him. He continued:

In your temporary failure there is no evidence that you may not yet be a better scholar, and a more successful man in the great struggle of life, than many others, who have entered college more easily.

Again I say let no feeling of discouragement prey upon you, and in the end you are sure to succeed.

George never did get into Harvard, but he did go to Yale.

On at least one occasion, Lincoln gave advice to a newly appointed judge about how best to perform his duties on the bench. "There is no mystery in this matter," Lincoln told him.

> *When you have a case between neighbors before you, listen well to all the evidence, stripping yourself of all prejudice, if any you have, and throwing away if you can all technical law knowledge, hear the lawyers make their arguments as patiently as you can, and after the evidence and the lawyers' arguments are through, then stop one moment and ask yourself: What is the justice in this case? and let that sense of justice be your decision. Law is nothing else but the best reason of wise men applied for ages to the transactions and business of mankind.*

Lincoln's advice on how to become a great lawyer is as useful today as it was when he gave it more than 150 years ago. Reading the books, studying the cases, understanding the principles, working diligently, and persevering in the face of adversity remain important keys to becoming successful at the bar.

This photograph, taken in Springfield on August 13, 1860, depicts Lincoln as a candidate for the presidency. It is believed to be the last portrait taken of the beardless Lincoln. Courtesy of the Library of Congress.

CHAPTER 2

"RESOLVE TO BE HONEST AT ALL EVENTS"

Lincoln's Character as a Lawyer

L AWYERS IN LINCOLN'S day had a reputation for being unscrupulous and
greedy, just as they often do today. As a consequence, Lincoln sought to instill in young
lawyers a sense of moral dignity in their profession. In a speech he composed in the early
1850s that he planned to deliver to aspiring
attorneys, he wrote:

> *There is a vague popular belief that lawyers
> are necessarily dishonest. I say vague, because
> when we consider to what extent confidence*

and honors are reposed in and conferred upon lawyers by the people, it appears improbable that their impression of dishonesty is very distinct and vivid. Yet the impression is common, almost universal. Let no young man choosing the law for a calling for a moment yield to the popular belief—resolve to be honest at all events; and if in your own judgment you cannot be an honest lawyer, resolve to be honest without being a lawyer. Choose some other occupation, rather than one in the choosing of which you do, in advance, consent to be a knave.

Lincoln's reputation for honesty is well deserved. His actions as a lawyer mirrored his everyday life. He acted with integrity and logic; he placed an emphasis on reason; and he called on Americans to maintain a reverence for the law at almost any cost. John H. Littlefield, who had worked in Lincoln's law office, recalled how Lincoln might reject a client whose case seemed dubious:

All clients knew that, with "Old Abe" as their lawyer, they would win their case—if it was fair; if not, that it was a waste of time to take it to him. After listening some time one day to a would-be client's statement, with his eyes on the ceiling, he swung around in his chair and exclaimed: "Well, you have a pretty good case in technical law, but a pretty bad one in equity and justice. You'll have to get some other fellow to win this case for you. I couldn't do it. All the time while standing talking to that jury I'd be thinking, 'Lincoln, you're a liar,' and I believe I should forget myself and say it out loud."

Lincoln's private secretaries, John Hay and John G. Nicolay, concurred:

He would have nothing to do with the "tricks" of the profession, though he met these readily enough when practised by others. He never knowingly undertook a case in which justice was on the side of his opponent. That same inconvenient honesty which prompted him, in his store-keeping days, to close the shop and go in search of a woman he had innocently defrauded of a few ounces of tea while weighing out her groceries, made it impossible for him to do his best with a poor case. "Swett," he once exclaimed [to his friend Leonard Swett], turning suddenly to his associate, "the man is guilty; you defend him—I can't," and gave up his share of a large fee.

This "inconvenient honesty" of Lincoln's even revealed itself in his facial expressions and body language. On another occasion, upon learning that his client was guilty, Lincoln turned to Swett again and said, "You speak to the jury. If I say a word, they will see from my face that the man is guilty and convict him." Once Lincoln apparently even walked out of the courtroom when he learned that his client was guilty. When a court officer came to retrieve him, he allegedly replied, "Tell the judge that my hands are dirty and I've gone away to wash them."

Many of Lincoln's associates noticed this same pattern—that he would reject clients he saw as greedy, dishonest, or in the wrong. Perhaps none learned this better than Lincoln's law partner, William H. Herndon. Once Herndon wanted Lincoln to take a case that Lincoln had doubts about. "Is this founded on fact?" Lincoln asked. Herndon was forced to admit that it was not. "You know it is a sham," Lincoln retorted, "and a sham is very often but another name for a lie. Don't let it go on record. The cursed thing may come staring us in the face long after this suit has been forgotten."

Herndon remembered these lessons for the rest of his life. Shortly after Lincoln's death in 1865, in a lecture titled "An Analysis of the Character of Abraham Lincoln," Herndon recalled Lincoln's thought process in selecting cases:

*The usual if not universal practice of Mr.
Lincoln was to closely and critically examine
his clients case—not ignoring even a just criti-
cism of his clients motives. If it was simply a
neighborhood quarrel—if it was a suit engen-
dered by hate, ill will and malice, a pig being
the occasion for its bursting out—if it was
simply a fight of keen avarice over a dollar he
could feel no interest in any or all such cases,
and generally put his iron face against them.*

Herndon declared that Lincoln was
"always...just and conscientious" toward his
clients. Even more important, Lincoln would
use his role as a lawyer to instill values in
potential clients.

*A gentleman would come into Mr. Lincoln's
office and state his case; and if the man's case
was a wrong, malicious bad case, Mr. Lincoln
would say—"My friend you are in the
wrong—You have no justice and no equity with*

you—I would advise you to drop the matter and fling away all thought of it to the winds."…

If a gentleman came into Mr. Lincoln's office and stated his case, and if he had the right side Mr. Lincoln told him he had the right and the equity. He then again patiently listened to what could be proved, and after forming his final opinion of the full whole merits of the case, he would say, "My friend—you are in the right but I don't think your evidences are sufficiently strong, always allowing a little for exaggerations, when so made—to drive conviction home to the minds of the jury: I advise you to compromise; and if you can't get this and can't find other and further proofs, I advise you to drop the case and fling away all thought of it to the winds."…

If a man came into his office and made a statement of his case and after patiently listening to the whole full story & points, including evidences—and proofs, if he formed the opinion that his client was right he said—"My friend you are in the right—can so demonstrate it to the minds of the jury—send home the conviction to the mind of the court [of] its legality and its justice. I have no reasonable doubt of this, but I advise you as a good man to go to your neighbor and say to him what you have done and ask him kindly but firmly to do justice & right. Then if he will not do it I'll make him," and when this was said there was no failure in the end.

Herndon concluded, "Mr. Lincoln was an extremely strong man when in the Right— the most sincere & powerful man I ever saw. His sincerity was all over his face, integrity & honor were there." Indeed, being on the right side of a case appears to have been more important to Lincoln than winning.

Many who practiced in the Illinois courts noticed Lincoln's penchant for justice, reason, and logic. John D. Caton, a justice on the Illinois Supreme Court who heard many of Lincoln's arguments, recalled:

Without the advantage of that mental culture which is afforded by a classical education, he learned the law as a science. Nature endowed him with a philosophical mind, and he learned and appreciated the elementary principles of the law and the reasons why they had become established as such. He remembered well what he read, because he fully comprehended it. He understood the relations of things, and hence his deductions were rarely wrong from any given state of facts. So he applied the principles of the law to the transactions of men with great clearness and precision. He was a close reasoner. He reasoned by analogy and usually enforced his views by apt illustrations... If he discovered a weak point in his case he frankly admitted it, and thereby prepared the mind to accept the more readily his mode of avoiding it.

Lincoln's unimpeachable honesty was also evident in how he treated his clients. Collecting attorney's fees could be a contentious matter.

Over the course of his career, Lincoln developed principles for determining the kinds of fees he would collect. He believed in treating his clients fairly and would not charge exorbitant fees. As a veteran attorney in the 1850s, he advised young lawyers:

> *The matter of fees is important, far beyond the mere question of bread and butter involved. Properly attended to, fuller justice is done to both lawyer and client. An exorbitant fee should never be claimed. As a general rule never take your whole fee in advance, nor any more than a small retainer. When fully paid beforehand, you are more than a common mortal if you can feel the same interest in the case, as if something was still in prospect for you, as well as for your client. And when you lack interest in the case the job will very likely lack skill and diligence in the performance. Settle the amount of fee and take a note in advance. Then you will feel that you*

are working for something, and you are sure to do your work faithfully and well. Never sell a fee note—at least not before the consideration service is performed. It leads to negligence and dishonesty—negligence by losing interest in the case, and dishonesty in refusing to refund when you have allowed the consideration to fail.

Lincoln strove to be fair in all of his dealings with clients. When he drew up papers for the leasing of a hotel in Quincy, Illinois, his client, George P. Floyd, sent him twenty-five dollars in payment. Lincoln replied to Floyd in a letter on February 21, 1856:

Dear Sir:

I have just received yours of 16th, with check on Flagg & Savage for twenty-five dollars. You must think I am a high-priced man. You are too liberal with your money. Fifteen dollars is enough for the job. I send

you a receipt for fifteen dollars, and return
to you a ten-dollar bill. Yours truly,

A. Lincoln

Nevertheless, Lincoln worked hard for his
clients and sometimes had to pursue them
for payment. Once, after winning a significant case for the Illinois Central Railroad,
he had to sue the railroad company for his
five-thousand-dollar fee (this was one of at
least seventeen times he sued a client for non-
payment). He and Stephen T. Logan apparently grew frustrated with clients who did not
pay their legal fees. On November 2, 1842,
Lincoln sent the following note to James S.
Irwin, another attorney in Springfield:

Judge Logan & myself are willing to
attend to any business in the Supreme
Court you may send us. As to fees, it is
impossible to establish a rule that will

apply in all, or even a great many cases. We believe we are never accused of being very unreasonable in this particular; and we would always be easily satisfied, provided we could see the money—but whatever fees we earn at a distance, if not paid *before*, we have noticed we never hear of after the work is done. We therefore, are growing a little sensitive on that point.

Yours &c.
A. Lincoln

But even when pursuing a client for non-payment, Lincoln's lighter side could still shine through. On July 4, 1851, Lincoln sent the following note to Andrew McCallen, which smacked of his backcountry humor:

Dear Sir:

I have news from Ottawa, that we *win*

our Galatin & Saline county case. As the dutch Justice said, when he married folks "Now, vere ish my hundred tollars" Yours truly

A. Lincoln

Some Americans today may believe that Lincoln was honest to a fault—but it was his integrity that earned him the trust and confidence of his neighbors. He used his reputation to build a successful law practice and political career, eventually reaching the nation's highest political office. It is little wonder that he still comes down to us today as "Honest Abe."

FOLLOWING HIS SINGLE TERM IN CONGRESS, LINCOLN
ARGUED A CASE IN 1849 BEFORE THE U.S. SUPREME
COURT (SEE CHAPTER 6). THIS IS THE FIRST PAGE OF HIS
HANDWRITTEN NOTES FOR THE ORAL ARGUMENT IN THAT
CASE, *LEWIS V. LEWIS*. COURTESY OF THE COLLECTION
OF THE SUPREME COURT OF THE UNITED STATES.

CHAPTER 3

"DISCOURAGE LITIGATION"

Lincoln's Advice to His Clients

A BRAHAM LINCOLN SAW the law as a noble—inherently moral—profession. He believed that lawyers should not practice law only for their own welfare and their clients' benefit, but also for the good of the community. His private secretaries, John Hay and John G. Nicolay, remarked years after his death, "Lincoln climbed this path for twenty-five years, with industry, perseverance, patience—above all, with that self-control and keen sense of right and wrong which always clearly traced the dividing line between his duty to his client and his duty to society and truth." Lincoln the lawyer is often described as a peacemaker. In contrast to some attorneys today, he sought to encourage his clients to resolve their troubles without resorting to litigation.

In the 1850s, Lincoln thought he might be able to earn supplemental income by giving lectures on various subjects. He delivered lectures on inventions and agriculture, and he drafted notes for a lecture on law (although he never delivered the lecture). His advice for young lawyers was drawn from his experience as a practicing attorney:

> *Discourage litigation. Persuade your neighbors to compromise whenever you can. Point out to them how the nominal winner is often a real loser—in fees, expenses, and waste of time. As a peacemaker the lawyer has a superior opportunity of being a good man. There will still be business enough.*

Never stir up litigation. A worse man can scarcely be found than one who does this. Who can be more nearly a fiend than he who habitually overhauls the register of deeds in search of defects in titles, whereon to stir up strife, and put money in his pocket? A moral tone ought to be infused into the profession which should drive such men out of it.

Those who knew Lincoln well knew that he practiced what he preached. Years after Lincoln died, John Foutch recalled an incident when he had tried to persuade Lincoln to serve as his counsel for a case:

I was a young man, just turned twenty-one. I had bought up some cattle, delivery to be made a few days later. Before the time came, the price of cattle went up and the man refused to deliver the consignment I had purchased. I decided to see my lawyer. That lawyer was Abraham Lincoln. He had always been my father's attorney. I found him in front of his flat-top desk, doing some writing.

"Sit down, John," said he and went on with his writing. When he had finished he turned, "Well, John, what is it?"

I stated my case.

Mr. Lincoln listened, shook his head, nodded—then spoke, "Yes, John, I think you have a meritorious case. You can sue the man and win, all right."

He sat still a while.

"John, how old are you?"

"Twenty-one," I replied.

"This your first lawsuit?"

"Yes, sir."

"John, don't have it. Don't have it. If you start out and win this suit, you will be running to me for a lawsuit every time any little disagreement comes up. John, don't have it. John, you go on home."

John Foutch concluded his story, "I went."

Lincoln sought to help his clients see the big picture—especially in cases that involved small matters. In an 1850 case involving wheat, he advised a client, "I sincerely hope you will settle it. I think you can if you will, for I have always found Mr. [Virgil] Hickox a fair man in his dealings... By settling, you will most likely get your money sooner; and with much less trouble & expense." On another occasion, he told a man who wanted to institute a suit over a pittance that he should drop the matter. "My friend," he told the angry client, "if you are going into the business of showing up every rascal you meet, you will have no time to do anything else the rest of your life."

A man once came to Lincoln with a case in which he sought 600 dollars. Lincoln told him:

Yes, there is no reasonable doubt but that I can gain your case for you. I can set a whole neighborhood at loggerheads; I can distress a

widowed mother and her six fatherless chil-
dren, and thereby gain for you six hundred
dollars, which rightfully belongs, it appears
to me, as much to them as it does to you. I
shall not take your case, but I will give you a
little advice for nothing. You seem a sprightly,
energetic man. I would advise you to try your
hand at making six hundred dollars in some
other way.

Lincoln, in short, used the practice of the law to serve as a peacemaker among neighbors.

Gibson W. Harris, a law student in the office of Lincoln and Herndon from 1845 to 1847, remembered how Lincoln would address potential clients:

Don't give me your strong points; they will
take care of themselves. Tell me your weak
points, and after that I can advise you what is
best to be done.

This advice often entailed compromising out of court. "I believe it literally true," stated Harris, "that by his counsel more cases were settled without trial than through litigation."

Of course, some cases could not be avoided. Lincoln handled more than one hundred divorce cases during his career. Perhaps these, more than any others, were the kinds of cases he would have liked to resolve out of court. He once quipped that divorce cases were not always safe for a lawyer to take:

I learned a great many years ago, that in a fight between a man and wife, a third party should never get between the woman's skillet and the man's ax-helve.

Americans today often lament the litigiousness of their society. Although it may seem quaint, Lincoln's advice to compromise and seek amicable results out of court may be a refreshing alternative to the prevalence of litigation we see every day in the news. Remarkably, Lincoln often did not even accept a fee when he could settle a case out of court. He told one client in 1850, "If you settle, I will charge nothing for what I have done, and thank you to boot." Law student Gibson W. Harris remembered Lincoln joking that he could not charge a fee in a case he settled out of court even if he wanted to. "They won't care to pay me," Lincoln cracked. "They don't think I have earned a fee unless I take the case into court and make a speech or two."

This illustration of "The Present Law Office
of Abraham Lincoln, the President Elect, on
Fifth Street, West Side of the Public Square,
Springfield, Illinois," appeared in *Frank Leslie's
Illustrated Newspaper* on December 22, 1860.
Courtesy of the Abraham Lincoln Presidential
Library and Museum.

CHAPTER 4

"LEAVE NOTHING FOR TO-MORROW WHICH CAN BE DONE TO-DAY"

Lincoln's Preparation for Trial

L INCOLN TOLD ASPIRING lawyers that they would have to work hard if they expected to succeed in the study and practice of the law. As a lawyer, Lincoln was widely reputed for being a diligent worker. His second law partner, Stephen T. Logan, remembered what Lincoln was like when he first met him and how Lincoln worked to prepare for a case:

Lincoln's knowledge of law was very small when I took him in. There were no books out

*here in those days worth speaking of. I don't
think he studied very much. I think he learned
his law more in the study of cases. He would
work hard and learn all there was in a case he
had in hand. He got to be a pretty good lawyer
though his general knowledge of law was never
very formidable. But he would study out his
case and make about as much of it as anybody.*

Logan's somewhat disparaging remarks may
have been an overstatement. But even Lincoln
could be modest and introspective about
his own skills and abilities. In the lecture he
drafted on the law, Lincoln opened humbly:

*I am not an accomplished lawyer. I find quite
as much material for a lecture in those points
wherein I have failed, as in those wherein I
have been moderately successful. The lead-
ing rule for the lawyer, as for the man of
every other calling, is diligence. Leave nothing for to-morrow which can be done to-day.*

Never let your correspondence fall behind. Whatever piece of business you have in hand, before stopping, do all the labor pertaining to it which can then be done. When you bring a common-law suit, if you have the facts for doing so, write the declaration at once. If a law point be involved, examine the books, and note the authority you rely on upon the declaration itself, where you are sure to find it when wanted. The same of defenses and pleas. In business not likely to be litigated,—ordinary collection cases, foreclosures, partitions, and the like,—make all examinations of titles, and note them, and even draft orders and decrees in advance. This course has a triple advantage; it avoids omissions and neglect, saves your labor when once done, performs the labor out of court when you have leisure, rather than in court when you have not.

One of the most important lessons Lincoln could teach young attorneys was to know exactly which fact or point of law was most important to convey to the judge or jury. In 1848, he advised a fellow Illinois attorney:

> In law it is good policy to never plead what you need *not*, lest you oblige yourself to prove what you can not. Reflect on this well before you proceed.

E. M. Prince of Bloomington, Illinois, heard Lincoln argue more than a hundred cases in court. He recalled that Lincoln "had a genius for seeing the real point in a case at once, and aiming steadily at it from the beginning of a trial to the end." While a "mediocre advocate" might be "apt to miss the crucial point in his case" and be "easily diverted with minor matters," Lincoln "instinctively saw the kernel of every case at the outset, never lost sight of it, and never let it escape the jury."

Another important lesson was to know his opponent's side better than his own. During the Civil War, Lincoln told Speaker of the House Schuyler Colfax that "a peculiarity of his own life from his earliest manhood had been, that he habitually studied the opposite side of every disputed question, of every law case, of every political issue, more exhaustively, if possible, than his own side. He said that the result had been, that in all his long practice at the bar he had never once been surprised in court by the strength of his adversary's case—often finding it much weaker than he had feared."

Along these lines, one of Lincoln's most powerful tactics in court was to concede points that he knew he could not win. His goal was to win the trust of the jury, all the while proving his most important points. "His perfect frankness of statement assured him the confidence of judge and jury in every argument," wrote private secretaries John Hay and John G. Nicolay. "His habit of fully admitting the weak points in his case gained him their close attention to his strong ones."

Many recognized this strategy in Lincoln's approach as a litigator, but some saw it as duplicitous. One Illinois lawyer noted that Lincoln had

> *the manner of treating his antagonist with such perfect fairness, as to make the jury and bystanders think that he could not be induced to take advantage of him—a manner which was the hell-firedest lie that was ever acted, because the very fairness he assumed was an ambuscade to cover up a battery, with which to destroy the opposing counsel, and so skillfully laid, too, that after it had done its work, only occasionally would the defeated party, and almost never would the uninitiated, discover the deception.*

This lawyer concluded that Lincoln's ability to persuade a jury in this way was "his very strongest weapon in the trial of a case."

Lincoln's friend Leonard Swett concurred:

As he entered the trial, where most lawyers object, he would say he "reckoned" it would be fair to let this in, or that; and sometimes when his adversary could not quite prove what Lincoln knew to be the truth, he would say he "reckoned" it would be fair to admit the truth to be so and so. When he did object to the court, after he heard his objections answered, he would often say: "Well, I reckon I must be wrong."

Now, about the time he had practiced this way about three-quarters through the case, if his adversary didn't understand him, he would wake up in a few moments, finding he had feared the Greeks too late, and wake up to find himself beaten. He was "wise as a serpent" in the trial of a case, but I have got too many scars from his blows to certify that he was "harmless as a dove." When the whole thing is unraveled the adversary begins to see that what he was so blandly giving away, was simply what he couldn't get and keep. By giving away six points and carrying the seventh, he carried his case, and, the whole case hanging on the seventh, he traded away everything which would give him the least aid in carrying that. Any one who took Lincoln for a simple-minded man would very soon wake up on his back, in a ditch.

But there were some exceptions to this rule. William H. Herndon recalled an 1859 case during which Lincoln apparently lost his temper. The judge refused to accept Lincoln's view of the law and overruled Lincoln's objection. But Lincoln refused to let the matter go.

Lincoln prepared himself well with law, came into court with an armful of books, and read the authorities plainly sustaining his view of the case... Lincoln could not stand the absurd decision, for it was absurd and without precedent in the broad world; and in his anger he rose up and seemed inspired with indignation,

mingled with a feeling of pity and contempt
for the judge's decision. He actually was fired
with indignation and spoke fiercely, strongly,
contemptuously of the decision of the Court.
Lincoln kept, in his anger and contempt,
just inside the walls of the law, did not do
anything, say anything, that would be a con-
tempt of court; he was careful and yet the
scoring that he gave the Court, through its
foolish decision, was terrible, blasting, crush-
ing, withering. I shall never forget the scene.
Lincoln had the crowd, the jury, the bar, in
perfect sympathy and accord. The Court's
decision was ridiculed, scoffed, and kicked
out of court. Lincoln was mad, vexed, and
indignant. When a great big man of mind
and body gets mad he is mad all over, terrible,
furious, eloquent, etc.

The judge finally relented and was either
"convinced or driven to pretend to believe"
that he had been wrong. Lincoln now "had

the field his own way, went to the jury, was able, eloquent, powerful" and won the case.

This last episode underscores the importance of never assuming that the judge or jury shares a common understanding of the law. Herndon recalled once doubting Lincoln's approach to an argument before the Illinois Supreme Court:

I heard him once argue a case and it was argued extremely well, it was logical, eloquent. In making his argument he referred to the history of the law, a useless part as I then thought. I know better now. After the speech was through and Lincoln had come into the law library room where the lawyers tell stories and prepare their cases, I said: "Lincoln, why did you go so far back in the history of the law as applicable to this case?" and to which he instantly replied: "I dare not trust this case on the presumptions that this court knows all things. I argued the case on the presumption that the court did not know anything."

Sometimes Lincoln sought to discern the opinion of the judge on a matter of law before entering the courtroom. Lincoln argued many cases in the Eighth Illinois Circuit before his close friend Judge David Davis—a man whom Lincoln would later appoint to the U.S. Supreme Court. Once when they were riding the circuit, Lincoln and Davis and several other lawyers were gathered together, chatting before a session of the court. Lincoln asked the group "a novel question regarding court practice" and was careful not to address the question to anyone in particular. Davis naturally gave his views on the subject. As one person who was present remembered:

Lincoln thereat laughed and said: "I asked that question, hoping that you would answer. I have that very question to present to the court in the morning, and I am very glad to find out that the court is on my side."

Ultimately, William H. Herndon maintained that the keys to Lincoln's success as a litigator could be summed up as follows:

Two things were essential to his success in managing a case. One was time; the other was feeling a confidence in the justice of the cause he represented. He used to say, "If I can free this case from technicalities and get it properly swung to the jury, I'll win it." But if either of these essentials were lacking, he was the weakest man at the bar.

If Lincoln had one other weakness as a lawyer, it was that he could be disorganized at times. He allowed his sons to run wild around his Springfield law office. Herndon later claimed, "If they pulled down all the books from the shelves, bent the points of all the pens, overturned inkstands, scattered law-papers over the floor, or threw the pencils in the spittoon, it never disturbed the serenity of their father's good nature... Had they s—t in Lincoln's hat and rubbed it on his boots, he would have laughed and thought it smart." The Lincoln boys got away with such hooliganism, Herndon said, because their father was so "frequently absorbed in thought" that "he never observed their mischievous but destructive pranks." Herndon did, but he chose to bite his tongue.

The disarray around Lincoln's office sometimes led him to fall behind on his correspondence with clients and fellow attorneys. As many people know today, he famously used his top hat as a file cabinet. In 1850, he once confessed to another lawyer:

I am ashamed of not sooner answering your letter, herewith returned; and, my only appologies are, first, that I have been very busy in the U.S. court; and second, that when I received the letter I put it in my old hat, and buying a new one the next day, the old one was set aside, and so, the letter [was] lost sight of for a time.

Fortunately, filing systems have improved over the past century and a half. Nevertheless, and despite these shortcomings, Lincoln proved a diligent advocate for his clients. He was always well prepared when he walked into the courtroom.

The Coles County Courthouse in Charleston, Illinois, in which Lincoln argued many cases. Courtesy of the Library of Congress.

CHAPTER 5

"ON RISING TO ADDRESS THE JURY"

Lincoln in the Courtroom

LINCOLN WAS A master when standing before a jury. He used stories, humor, exhibits, and pure logic to sway the men in the jury box to his side. His second law partner, Stephen T. Logan, recalled that Lincoln was skilled in "getting the good will of juries" by putting "himself at once on an equality with everybody." Another of Lincoln's associates reminisced, "A stranger going into a court when he was trying a case would after a few minutes find himself instinctively on Lincoln's side and wishing him success."

Lincoln had a knack for connecting with juries, just as though he were speaking with old friends in the neighborhood. His approach to public speaking exuded candor and integrity, and his honest disposition frequently won jurors over to his side. "He never talked long," remembered John Strong of Atlanta, Illinois. "In stating a disputed proposition he would say, not, 'This is the way it is,' but 'This is the way it seems to me,' thus allowing for an honest difference of opinion."

William H. Herndon recalled advice Lincoln had given him regarding how to address a jury:

Don't shoot too high. Aim lower, and the common people will understand you. They are the ones you want to reach—at least they are the ones you ought to reach. The educated and refined people will understand you, anyway. If you aim too high, your ideas will go over the heads of the masses and only hit those who need no hitting.

An old acquaintance from the Illinois legislature had a similar experience with Lincoln. "He had great natural clearness and simplicity of statement," said Joseph Gillespie. "He despised everything like ornament or display and confined himself to a dry bold statement of his point and then worked away with sledgehammer logic at making out his case." Another Illinois attorney praised Lincoln's ability to "disentangle" a complicated case "and present the real issue in so simple and clear a way that all could understand." This ability to be concise and clear was Lincoln's "great secret as an orator," recalled Leonard Swett:

When Lincoln had stated a case, it was always more than half argued and the point more than half won. The first impression he generally conveyed was, that he had stated the case of his adversary better and more forcibly, than his opponent could state it himself. He then answered that state of facts fairly and fully, never passing by, or skipping over a bad point. When this was done, he presented his own case. There was a feeling when he argued a case, in the mind of any man who listened to him, that nothing had been passed over... The force of his logic was in conveying to the minds of others the same clear and thorough analysis he had in his own, and if his own mind failed to be satisfied, he had no power to satisfy any body else.

Judge David Davis agreed: "He seized the strong points of a cause and presented them with clearness and great compactness. His mind was logical and direct, and he did not indulge in extraneous discussion."

Of equal importance, Lincoln had a way of being personable and sincere in the courtroom, making everyone feel comfortable around him. Dennis Hanks, a cousin of Lincoln's mother, recalled:

But he never was sassy or quarrelsome. I've
seen him walk into a crowd of sawin' rowdies,
and tell some droll yarn and bust them all up.
It was the same when he was a lawyer; all
eyes, whenever he riz were on him; there was
a suthin' peculiarsome *about him.*

Those who served on juries when Lincoln
was in the courtroom had similar recollections.
Felix Ryan of Lincoln, Illinois, remembered
having sat on juries in cases that Lincoln argued:

He knew nearly every juror, and when he
made his speech he talked to the jurors, one
at a time, like an old friend who wanted to
reason it out with them and make it as easy as
possible for them to find the truth.

Another juror similarly recalled: "Lincoln's
chief characteristics are candor, good nature,
and shrewdness. He is a gentleman throughout. I wish I could add—the scholar. He

possesses a noble heart, an elevated mind, and the true elements of politeness."

Lincoln treated witnesses in the same manner. James Hoblit recalled being on the witness stand during a cross-examination by Lincoln. Hoblit hoped "to say as little as possible" because he knew that his testimony could damage his uncle's case. He recalled:

Well, as soon as I told Mr. Lincoln my full name he became very much interested, asking me if I wasn't some relative of his old friend John Hoblit who kept the halfway house between Springfield and Bloomington; and when I answered that he was my grandfather, Mr. Lincoln grew very friendly, plying me with all sorts of questions about family matters, which put me completely at my ease, and before I knew what was happening, I had forgotten to be hostile and he had the whole story.

After the trial, Hoblit felt dejected for

having ruined his uncle's case. Lincoln saw him and said that "I had acted rightly and no one could criticize me for what I had done." Hoblit "never forgot his friendly and encouraging words at a time when I needed sympathy and consolation."

Lincoln's ability to get the testimony he needed from witnesses like Hoblit reflected his superior talents in cross-examination. "He was a great cross-examiner," stated Illinois lawyer James Ewing, "in that he never asked an unnecessary question. He knew when and where to stop with a witness, and when a man has learned that he is entitled to take rank as an expert questioner." One Illinois lawyer noted that Lincoln paid such careful attention to witnesses' statements that "he took no notes, but remembered everything quite as well as those who did so."

As a trial proceeded, Lincoln "moved cautiously," remembered Lawrence Weldon, "and never examined or cross-examined witnesses to the detriment of his own side. If the witness told the truth, he was safe from his attacks; but woe betide the unlucky or dishonest individual who suppressed the truth or colored it." Henry Clay Whitney concurred: "He understood human nature thoroughly, and was very expert and incisive in his cross-examination of witnesses. If a witness told the truth without evasion Lincoln was respectful and patronizing to him, but he would score a perjured witness unmercifully." Indeed, Lincoln's third law partner, William H. Herndon, stated, "Woe be to the man who hugged to his bosom a secret error if Abraham Lincoln ever set out to uncover it. All the ingenuity of delusive reasoning, all the legerdemain of debate, could hide it in no nook or angle of space in which he would not detect and expose it."

When addressing the courtroom, Lincoln controlled his tone and inflection in a way that made his speech engaging. His voice could be high and raspy, his pronunciation of words might sound backwoods and uneducated, and he did not always know what to do with his hands—his large, gangly, rail-splitting hands. But once he got going, Lincoln had a way of captivating his audience. A young man who heard him speak in New York City in 1860 described him as "awkwardness deified." William H. Herndon recalled in 1887:

On rising to address the jury or the crowd he quite generally placed his hands behind him, the back part of his left hand resting in the palm of his right hand. As he proceeded and grew warmer, he moved his hands to the front of his person, generally interlocking his fingers and running one thumb around the other. Sometimes his hands, for a short while, would hang by his side. In still growing warmer, as he proceeded in his address, he used his hands—especially and generally his right hand—in his gestures; he used his head a great deal in speaking, throwing or jerking or moving it now here and now there, now in this position and now in that, in order to be more emphatic, to drive the idea home. Mr. Lincoln never beat the air, never sawed space with his hands, never acted for stage effect: was cool, careful, earnest, sincere, truthful, fair, self-possessed, not insulting, not dictatorial; was pleasing, good-natured; had great strong naturalness of look, pose, and act; was clear in his ideas, simple in his words, strong, terse, and demonstrative; he spoke and acted to convince individuals and masses; he used in his gestures his right hand, sometimes shooting out that long bony forefinger of his to dot an idea or to express a thought, resting his thumb on his middle finger. Bear in mind that he did not gesticulate much and yet it is true that every organ of his body was in motion and acted with ease, elegance, and grace, so it all looked to me.

These sorts of skills do not come naturally to most public speakers. In his undelivered lecture on law, Lincoln advised young attorneys:

Extemporaneous speaking should be practised and cultivated. It is the lawyer's avenue to the public. However able and faithful he may be in other respects, people are slow to bring him business if he cannot make a speech. And yet there is not a more fatal error to young lawyers than relying too much on speech-making. If any one, upon his rare powers of speaking, shall claim an exemption from the drudgery of the law, his case is a failure in advance.

Lincoln also encouraged young attorneys to speak with sincerity and from the heart. During a criminal case in 1850, he proposed that a young lawyer named James Haines make the opening argument for the defense. Haines was nervous, but Lincoln put his hand on Haines's shoulder and said:

I want you to open the case, and when you are doing it, talk to the jury as though your client's fate depends on every word you utter. Forget that you have any one to fall back upon, and you will do justice to yourself and your client.

Lincoln understood the importance of avoiding dry legalese in the courtroom. He regaled his audiences with pithy stories, and judges and other lawyers often looked to Lincoln for a joke. He often spontaneously inserted his own light-hearted humor into a case. One time, when he was facing his former law partner, Stephen T. Logan, in court, Lincoln noticed that Logan's shirt was on backward. Lincoln sought to disarm Logan by a clever address to the jury:

Gentlemen, you must be careful and not permit yourselves to be overborne by the eloquence of the counsel for defense. Judge Logan, I know, is an effective lawyer; I have met him too often to doubt that; but shrewd and careful though he be, still he is sometimes wrong. Since this trial begun I have discovered that, with all his caution and fastidiousness, he hasn't knowledge enough to put his shirt on right.

According to an early twentieth-century account, "Logan turned crimson with embarrassment, and the jurors burst into a roar of laughter as they discovered that the discomfited advocate was wearing the garment in question with the plaited bosom behind, and for the rest of that trial Logan was not effective against his former partner."

Significantly, Lincoln's stories always had a point (which, according to Herndon, was sometimes just to keep the jury interested or awake). "In all my experience," said James Ewing, a boy whose father had owned a hotel where Lincoln boarded while traveling on the judicial circuit, "I never heard Mr. Lincoln tell a story for its own sake or simply to raise a laugh. He used stories to illustrate a point."

DAVID DAVIS (1815–1886) PRESIDED OVER THE EIGHTH
JUDICIAL CIRCUIT IN ILLINOIS FROM 1848 TO 1862. HE
WAS LINCOLN'S CAMPAIGN MANAGER AT THE REPUBLICAN
NATIONAL CONVENTION IN 1860, AND LATER SERVED AS
AN ASSOCIATE JUSTICE ON THE U.S. SUPREME COURT FROM
1862 TO 1877. COURTESY OF THE LIBRARY OF CONGRESS.

CHAPTER 6

"ALL THE LAWS BUT ONE"

A Lawyer in the White House

ABRAHAM LINCOLN ARGUED one case before the U.S. Supreme Court—a dry, technical case about statutes of limitations called *Lewis v. Lewis* in 1849. He lost, and Chief Justice Roger B. Taney wrote the Opinion of the Court. This little-known moment was just the first of several important encounters between the prairie lawyer from Illinois and the aged, proslavery judge from Maryland.

While Lincoln was arguing *Lewis v. Lewis* in the Supreme Court chamber in the basement of the Capitol, another much more important case was wending its way through the state and federal judicial systems. In the 1830s, a Missouri slave named Dred Scott had been taken onto free soil in Illinois and the Wisconsin Territory. In 1846, Scott sued his owner, claiming that he was now a free man. After losing his case in the state court system, Scott brought suit in a federal district court, but his case wasn't finally decided until 1857. In what might be the most notorious decision in Supreme Court history, Chief Justice Taney declared that African Americans were not citizens and could not sue in the federal courts.

Taney's sweeping pronouncement in *Dred Scott v. Sandford* was greeted with anger by many northerners. In a long speech delivered at Springfield, Illinois, on June 26, 1857, Lincoln said that he would "offer no resistance to" the decision, but that he and other Republicans would "do what we can" to have the Court "over-rule this" decision, which he believed was based on "partisan bias" and "assumed historical facts which are not really true."

In the wake of the *Dred Scott* decision, Lincoln feared the immense power of the Supreme Court to shape public policy. In his famous "House Divided" address in 1858, Lincoln expressed his anxiety that the Supreme Court would work with northern Democrats to hand down another decision making slavery a national institution.

Welcome or unwelcome, such decision is probably coming, and will soon be upon us, unless the power of the present political dynasty shall be met and overthrown. We shall lie down pleasantly dreaming that the people of Missouri are on the verge of making their State free; and we shall awake to the reality, instead, that the Supreme Court has made Illinois a slave State.

Lincoln was elected president in 1860, and the Civil War intervened before the Supreme Court could make the decision Lincoln feared. In a moment of great irony, none other than Chief Justice Taney administered the oath of office to Lincoln on March 4, 1861. Like all of his predecessors, Lincoln swore to "preserve, protect and defend the Constitution of the United States of America."

In his first inaugural address, Lincoln obliquely alluded to the *Dred Scott* case, telling the American people that the Supreme Court ought not to have the final say on all matters of public policy:

> *I do not forget the position assumed by some, that constitutional questions are to be decided by the Supreme Court; nor do I deny that such decisions must be binding in any case, upon the parties to a suit, as to the object of that suit, while they are also entitled to very high respect and consideration, in all paralel*

cases, by all other departments of the government. And while it is obviously possible that such decision may be erroneous in any given case, still the evil effect following it, being limited to that particular case, with the chance that it may be over-ruled, and never become a precedent for other cases, can better be borne than could the evils of a different practice. At the same time the candid citizen must confess that if the policy of the government, upon vital questions, affecting the whole people, is to be irrevocably fixed by decisions of the Supreme Court, the instant they are made, in ordinary litigation between parties, in personal actions, the people will have ceased, to be their own rulers, having, to that extent, practically resigned their government, into the hands of that eminent tribunal.

Lincoln did not see this view as "any assault upon the court or the judges," and he acknowledged that judges had "a duty from which they may not shrink to decide cases properly brought before them, and it is no fault of theirs if others seek to turn their decisions to political purposes." Still, in this first inaugural address, Lincoln laid the groundwork for the positions that he would take throughout the Civil War. He had a war to fight and win, and if the judiciary tried to hinder him, he would simply ignore the judges.

The first significant conflict between Lincoln and the judges arose in 1861 over the arrest of a Baltimore County farmer named John Merryman. As a state militia officer, Merryman had burned railroad bridges in April 1861 in an attempt to prevent federal troops from passing through Maryland on their way to Washington, DC. After federal authorities gained control of Baltimore, Union troops promptly arrested Merryman at his home on May 25 at 2 a.m. They rushed him to prison at Fort McHenry (the inspiration for the national anthem), and held him there without charges.

Merryman's lawyers petitioned Chief Justice Taney for a writ of habeas corpus—a court order that would require the arresting officer to justify the arrest of their client. But the military refused to bring the prisoner into Taney's courtroom. Instead, they informed the aged judge that Lincoln had suspended the writ of habeas corpus, citing the provision of the Constitution that permits the writ to be suspended "when in Cases of Rebellion or Invasion the public Safety may require it."

Chief Justice Taney was indignant. He issued an opinion blasting Lincoln for suspending the writ of habeas corpus, arguing that it was a legislative power, since the suspension clause is in Article I of the Constitution. Moreover, he chastised the president and the military for thrusting aside the civil courts and the Bill of Rights:

Such is the case now before me, and I can only say that if the authority which the constitution has confided to the judiciary department and judicial officers, may thus, upon any pretext or under any circumstances, be usurped by the military power, at its discretion, the people of the United States are no longer living under a government of laws, but every citizen holds life, liberty and property at the will and pleasure of the army officer in whose military district he may happen to be found.

The chief justice then added a stern admonition to the president:

I have exercised all the power which the constitution and laws confer upon me, but that power has been resisted by a force too strong for me to overcome… It will then remain for that high officer, in fulfillment of his constitutional obligation to "take care that the laws be faithfully executed," to determine what measures he will take to cause the civil process of the United States to be respected and enforced.

Lincoln, however, ignored Taney's opinion and continued to use the power of his office to arrest disloyal civilians, some of whom he brought to trial in military tribunals.

On July 4, 1861, Lincoln sent a message to Congress, reminding the nation that all of the laws were being resisted in a large part of the Union. He wondered whether those laws should all be allowed to fail even if he could preserve them by violating one single law "to a very limited extent... To state the question more directly," Lincoln continued, "are all the laws, *but one*, to go unexecuted, and the government itself go to pieces, lest that one be violated?" The implication was clear. It made sense to temporarily violate one law if doing so meant preserving the nation and all of its other laws. Still, Lincoln denied that he had acted illegally since the Constitution permits the writ to be suspended during a rebellion.

In a public letter in June 1863, Lincoln used a clever but homely metaphor to persuade the

American people of the justice of his actions, just as he had done while standing before jury boxes on countless other occasions earlier:

> Long experience has shown that armies can not be maintained unless desertion shall be punished by the severe penalty of death. The case requires, and the law and the constitution, sanction this punishment. Must I shoot a simple-minded soldier boy who deserts, while I must not touch a hair of a wiley agitator who induces him to desert?... I think that in such a case, to silence the agitator, and save the boy, is not only constitutional, but, withal, a great mercy.

Lincoln exercised extraordinary power in other ways during the war as well, and his skills as a lawyer often shone through. Initially, he refused to emancipate the slaves in the South, in part because he knew it

would be politically and militarily impru-
dent to do so too early in the war, and in
part because he knew that he was bound
to uphold the Constitution—a document
that protected slavery where it existed.
When he finally crafted the Emancipation
Proclamation during the summer of 1862,
he did so carefully so that it could with-
stand challenges in the courts. In 1864, he
explained his thinking on the constitutional-
ity of emancipation in a public letter to the
American people:

> I am naturally anti-slavery. If slavery
> is not wrong, nothing is wrong. I can not
> remember when I did not so think, and
> feel. And yet I have never understood
> that the Presidency conferred upon me
> an unrestricted right to act officially
> upon this judgment and feeling. It was in
> the oath I took that I would, to the best of
> my ability, preserve, protect, and defend

the Constitution of the United States. I could not take the office without taking the oath. Nor was it my view that I might take an oath to get power, and break the oath in using the power. I understood, too, that in ordinary civil administration this oath even forbade me to practically indulge my primary abstract judgment on the moral question of slavery. I had publicly declared this many times, and in many ways. And I aver that, to this day, I have done no official act in mere deference to my abstract judgment and feeling on slavery.

By the midpoint of the war, however, Lincoln explained that he had come to understand that destroying slavery had become "indispensable" to preserving the nation and the Constitution. Using another homespun yet lawyerly metaphor, Lincoln sought to persuade Americans that emancipating southern slaves had become lawful, even though earlier in the war he had claimed it was not:

I did understand however, that my oath to preserve the constitution to the best of my ability, imposed upon me the duty of preserving, by every indispensable means, that government—that nation—of which that constitution was the organic law. Was it possible to lose the nation, and yet preserve the constitution? By general law life and limb must be protected; yet often a limb must be amputated to save a life; but a life is never wisely given to save a limb. I felt that measures, otherwise unconstitutional, might become lawful, by becoming indispensable to the preservation of the constitution, through the preservation of the nation. Right or wrong, I assumed this ground, and now avow it. I could not feel that, to the best of my ability, I had even tried to preserve the constitution, if, to save slavery, or any minor matter, I should permit the wreck of government, country, and Constitution all together.

Many of Lincoln's constitutional decisions were controversial during the war—some even remain so 150 years later. When the time came for Lincoln to make appointments to the Supreme Court, he wanted nominees whom he could trust to uphold his policies and constitutional principles. In 1864, when given the opportunity to replace Roger B. Taney as chief justice of the United States, Lincoln is said to have remarked:

We wish for a Chief Justice who will sustain what has been done in regard to emancipation and the legal tenders. We cannot ask a man what he will do, and if we should, and he should answer us, we should despise him for it. Therefore, we must take a man whose opinions are known.

Lincoln appointed five men to the Supreme Court—two of whom were very well known to him. For chief justice, Lincoln appointed his former secretary of the treasury, Salmon P. Chase. Chase had been vying for the presidency for years. Perhaps Lincoln thought he might be satisfied with a life-tenured seat at the center of the Supreme Court's bench.

One of Lincoln's other appointments was David Davis, the three-hundred-pound judge from Illinois's Eighth Judicial Circuit. Over the previous two decades, Lincoln had followed Davis from town to town, arguing cases before the rotund jurist. On some occasions, Lincoln even filled in for him as a judge (Lincoln presided over ninety-five cases in 1858 alone). In 1860, Davis served as Lincoln's campaign manager at the Republican National Convention. Lincoln rewarded his old friend with a seat on the Supreme Court in 1862.

While Lincoln and Davis were old friends

and Republican Party stalwarts, they did not always see eye to eye on all issues. Throughout the war, Davis was critical of Lincoln's suspension of habeas corpus and use of military tribunals to try civilians, but he kept his views to himself. On a few occasions he sent private letters to the president expressing his concerns, but he refused to publicly undermine Lincoln's decisions in his capacity as a judge.

Following the war, however—and after Lincoln's death—Judge Davis took the opportunity to declare Lincoln's use of military courts to try civilians unconstitutional in a case called *Ex parte Milligan* (1866). Davis maintained that the rights to personal liberty guaranteed in the Constitution had to be protected, even amid the tumult of civil war. Nevertheless, Davis praised his old friend from Springfield, comparing him to George Washington:

This nation, as experience has proved,

cannot always remain at peace, and has no right to expect that it will always have wise and humane rulers sincerely attached to the principles of the Constitution. Wicked men, ambitious of power, with hatred of liberty and contempt of law, may fill the place once occupied by Washington and Lincoln, and if this right is conceded, and the calamities of war again befall us, the dangers to human liberty are frightful to contemplate. If our fathers had failed to provide for just such a contingency, they would have been false to the trust reposed in them. They knew—the history of the world told them—the nation they were founding, be its existence short or long, would be involved in war; how often or how long continued human foresight could not tell, and that unlimited power, wherever lodged at such a time, was especially hazardous to freemen. For this and other equally weighty reasons, they secured the inheritance they had fought to maintain by incorporating in a written constitution the safeguards which time had proved were essential to its preservation.

The tension between individual liberty and national security was palpable during the Civil War. Lincoln went to great and controversial lengths to win the war. As a consequence, his tenure as president was one of the most contentious in our history. Nevertheless, it is important to understand why Lincoln believed that preserving the Union was so important. For Lincoln, the nation was worth fighting for—even at great cost—because a Union victory would prove to the world that ordinary men and women could govern themselves as a free people under a system of laws. The Declaration of Independence, Lincoln said, "gave promise that in due time the weights should be lifted from the shoulders of all men, and that all should have an equal chance." Such a national ideal was worth fighting for, as Lincoln famously proclaimed at Gettysburg, so "that government of the people, by the people, for the people, shall not perish from the earth."

Lincoln with his son Tad, taken at Mathew Brady's Gallery in Washington, DC, on February 9, 1864. Courtesy of the Library of Congress.

"REVERENCE FOR THE LAWS"

D ESPITE THE CONTROVERSIES of his presidency, Lincoln viewed adherence to the law as the best way to preserve the blessings of liberty for future generations. In January 1838—when he was still in his twenties—he delivered one of the most remarkable speeches of his life to the Young Men's Lyceum in Springfield. America was sinking into a period of mob violence and vigilante justice. Lincoln called on his audience to reject such an unjust approach to criminal justice and to cling to the values and institutions established by the nation's Founding Fathers.

"I hope I am over wary," he said, but "the increasing disregard for law," which he could see pervading the country, was substituting "the wild and furious passions" of "savage mobs" for "the sober judgment of Courts." Lincoln feared that "if the laws be continually despised and disregarded" that the rights of the people would be insecure, and that the people would lose their "affection" for the greatest government that had ever been established on the earth. He counseled his listeners to remember the sacrifices of the Revolutionary generation so that they would value the institutions that that generation had created. Moreover, he admonished Americans to instill reverence for the law in all succeeding generations.

The answer is simple. Let every American, every lover of liberty, every well wisher to his posterity, swear by the blood of the Revolution, never to violate in the least particular, the laws of the country; and never to tolerate their violation by others. As the patriots of seventy-six did to the support of the Declaration of Independence, so to the support of the Constitution and Laws, let every American pledge his life, his property, and his sacred honor;—let every man remember that to violate the law, is to trample on the blood of his father, and to tear the character of his own, and his children's liberty. Let reverence for the laws, be breathed by every American mother, to the lisping babe, that prattles on her lap—let it be taught in schools, in seminaries, and in colleges—let it be written in Primers, spelling books, and in Almanacs;—let it be preached from the pulpit, proclaimed in legislative halls, and enforced in courts of justice. And, in short, let it become the political religion of the nation; and let the old and the young, the

*rich and the poor, the grave and the gay, of
all sexes and tongues, and colors and condi-
tions, sacrifice unceasingly upon its altars.*

Lincoln had been practicing law for less
than a year when he delivered this speech, but
his ardent adherence to law and order stuck
with him for the rest of his life. As he traveled to Washington, DC, as president-elect in
1861, Lincoln stopped at Independence Hall
in Philadelphia to raise a flag on February
22—George Washington's birthday. Lincoln
had recently learned that there was a credible
threat against his life in Baltimore, a city he
would be passing through on February 23.
Still, he spoke boldly at Independence Hall
about the importance of adhering to America's
founding principles. "I have never had a feeling politically that did not spring from the
sentiments embodied in the Declaration of
Independence," he declared in an impromptu
speech. And he maintained that if the nation

could not be saved without preserving the principles of the Declaration, "it will be truly awful." Speaking extemporaneously, he continued, "But, if this country cannot be saved without giving up that principle—I was about to say I would rather be assassinated on this spot than to surrender it."

Lincoln did die by an assassin's hand just four short years later as he fought to preserve government by consent and liberty under law.

A NOTE ON SOURCES

M ANY BOOKS HAVE been written about
Abraham Lincoln; only a few deal
extensively with his practice as a lawyer. The
early ten-volume biography *Abraham Lincoln:
A History* (New York: Century, 1890), published by his private secretaries, John Hay
and John G. Nicolay, includes a number of
wonderful stories, as do the interviews and
letters collected by Lincoln's last law partner,
William H. Herndon. Herndon's anecdotes
can be found in several sources, most notably in Douglas L. Wilson and Rodney O.
Davis, *Herndon's Informants: Letters, Interviews,
and Statements about Abraham Lincoln* (Urbana:
University of Illinois Press, 1998), Emanuel
Hertz, *The Hidden Lincoln: From the Letters*

and Papers of William H. Herndon (New York: Blue Ribbon Books, 1940), William H. Herndon and Jesse W. Weik, *Herndon's Life of Lincoln* (New York: Da Capo Press, 1983), and Harold Holzer, ed., *Lincoln as I Knew Him: Gossip, Tributes and Revelations from His Best Friends and Worst Enemies* (Chapel Hill, NC: Algonquin Books, 1999).

Readers who wish to see more of Lincoln's words firsthand should consult the nine-volume *The Collected Works of Abraham Lincoln*, edited by Roy P. Basler (New Brunswick, NJ: Rutgers University Press, 1953–1955). Words attributed to Lincoln by those who knew him can be found in Don E. Fehrenbacher and Virginia Fehrenbacher, eds., *Recollected Words of Abraham Lincoln* (Stanford: Stanford University Press, 1996). Highlights from Lincoln's writings are available in Gordon Leidner, ed., *Abraham Lincoln: Quotes, Quips, and Speeches* (Nashville, TN: Cumberland House, 2009).

Much of Lincoln's personal correspondence has been digitized by the Library of Congress and is available at memory.loc.gov/. Many papers from his law practice are available in Daniel W. Stowell et al., eds., *The Papers of Abraham Lincoln: Legal Documents and Cases,* 4 vols. (Charlottesville: University of Virginia Press, 2008), and are also available online at www.lawpracticeofabraham lincoln.org/.

A collection of essays entitled *Abraham Lincoln, Esq.: The Legal Career of America's Greatest President* (Lexington: University Press of Kentucky, 2010), which was edited by Roger Billings and former Rhode Island Chief Justice Frank J. Williams, contains chapters on various aspects of Lincoln's legal practice. A sparkling essay by Harold Holzer opens the book by describing how Lincoln's reputation as a lawyer has risen and fallen over the years since his death. Readers may also wish to consult Frederick Trevor Hill's

Lincoln the Lawyer (New York: Century, 1913), John Lupton's "Basement Barrister: Abraham Lincoln's Practice before the United States Supreme Court," *Lincoln Herald* 101 (June 1999): 47–58, and Brian R. Dirck's *Lincoln the Lawyer* (Urbana: University of Illinois Press, 2007).

Two recent biographies explore Lincoln's career as a lawyer in some detail. Michael Burlingame's two-volume *Abraham Lincoln: A Life* (Baltimore: Johns Hopkins University Press, 2009), contains nearly every known story related to Lincoln's life, including his practice as a lawyer. Allen C. Guelzo's *Abraham Lincoln: Redeemer President* (Grand Rapids, MI: Eerdmans, 1999), nicely captures Lincoln's career as a frontier attorney seeking to build his career, reputation, and clientele. Both biographies won the prestigious Lincoln Prize.

Lincoln's career as a lawyer in the White House has been explored in several books, most notably Mark E. Neely Jr.'s Pulitzer

Prize–winning *The Fate of Liberty: Abraham Lincoln and Civil Liberties* (New York: Oxford University Press, 1991), Phillip Shaw Paludan's *The Presidency of Abraham Lincoln* (Lawrence: University Press of Kansas, 1994), Daniel A. Farber's *Lincoln's Constitution* (Chicago: University of Chicago Press, 2003), James F. Simon's *Lincoln and Chief Justice Taney: Slavery, Secession, and the President's War Powers* (New York: Simon and Schuster, 2006), Brian McGinty's *Lincoln and the Court* (Cambridge, MA: Harvard University Press, 2008), and my own *Abraham Lincoln and Treason in the Civil War: The Trials of John Merryman* (Baton Rouge: Louisiana State University Press, 2011). Readers interested in Lincoln's dealing with the Sioux uprising of 1862 should read Ron Soodalter's excellent piece published at the *New York Times* "Disunion" blog on August 20, 2012.

INDEX

ACKNOWLEDGMENTS

I HAD THE IDEA for this book when I became prelaw advisor at Christopher Newport University in October 2012. As I worked with my students in their preparations for law school—and also was thinking about Lincoln's life and character in my own research—I realized that Lincoln still had a lot to say about what it means to be a good lawyer, even 150 years after his death.

I thank my students Ben Coffman, Erin Bello, and Lizzy Wall for assistance in tracking down some of the stories in this book. Ben, who is now a law student at the University of Virginia, also read an early version of the book and offered very helpful advice.

Matthew Hofstedt of the Curator's Office

at the Supreme Court of the United States provided information related to Lincoln and the Court. John Lupton, an expert on Lincoln's legal career and executive director of the Illinois Supreme Court Historic Preservation Commission, and Harold Holzer, senior vice president for public affairs at the Metropolitan Museum of Art and the author of many wonderful books on Lincoln, both read the entire manuscript and provided very helpful comments.

I thank my mom, Eileen White, for reading through this manuscript, as she has done with every book I've written. My wife, Lauren, my in-laws, Dave and Leigh Kramer, and my good friend Ian Drake, who is a professor of jurisprudence at Montclair State University, also all read through the book and offered valuable suggestions.

Finally, I thank Jenna Skwarek, Ariel Bronson, Becca Sage, and Stephanie Bowen of Sourcebooks for their support of this project, and Gordon Leidner—a fellow board member of the Abraham Lincoln Institute—for putting me in contact with Sourcebooks.

ABOUT THE AUTHOR

J ONATHAN W. WHITE teaches American studies at Christopher Newport University, where he also serves as prelaw advisor. Prior to joining the faculty at CNU, he worked

as an assistant historian at the Federal Judicial Center in Washington, DC. He has published several other books, including *Abraham Lincoln and Treason in the Civil War: The Trials of John Merryman* (2011) and *Emancipation, the Union Army, and the Reelection of Abraham Lincoln* (2014). He has written more than two dozen articles in scholarly journals and popular history magazines, and has won a number of prizes, including the 2005 John T. Hubbell Prize for the best article in *Civil War History*, the 2010 Hay-Nicolay Prize for the best dissertation on Lincoln and the Civil War, and the 2012 Thomas Jefferson Prize for his *Guide to Research in Federal Judicial History* (2010). He serves on the board of directors of the Abraham Lincoln Institute, and is a member of the Abraham Lincoln Association and the Lincoln Forum.

For more information, please visit: www.jonathanwhite.org.